From the Middle Country

From the Middle Country

tanka by Noriko Tanaka
translated by Amelia Fielden
and Saeko Ogi

From the Middle Country
ISBN 978 1 74027 908 6
Copyright © tanka Noriko Tanaka
Copyright © translation Amelia Fielden & Saeko Ogi 2015

First published 2015 by
GINNINDERRA PRESS
PO Box 3461 Port Adelaide 5015 Australia
www.ginninderrapress.com.au

Contents

Foreword	7
I From the Ocean Country: Blue Times	11
II From the Middle Country: Onogoro Island	21
III From the Country of the Dead: The Sleeping River	32
Afterword	61
Noriko Tanaka: A Brief Biography	62

Foreword

This is a book of remarkable tanka by a remarkable poet. Noriko Tanaka writes within the ancient traditions of tanka yet transforms the voice of that poetry into an instrument wholly in tune with modern life and the introspections of an intelligent, sensitive, contemporary woman in whom we may recognise something of ourselves. All this is accomplished in the magic and elasticity of her imagery, phrasing and often startling interior dialogue with herself.

Within their clusters and groupings, Tanaka's tanka interact with each other in oblique but effective ways. In their proximity, the poems transform and blend into new, unexpected dimensions. The poet deftly creates patterns from interweaving elements and the secondary meanings of the words, building upon imagery, phrases, and specific details that reflect, echo and beautifully balance one another without any actual repetition. This movement, I find, is analogous to the variations of theme and musical phrase found in a sonata.

We may occasionally feel especially challenged to keep up with the imaginative leaps Tanaka makes between one subject and another. Idea and image, as well as sound and sense, may seem to whirl within each short song, and between or among songs to move outward at times, inward at other times, having the effect of a vortex that pulls us into Tanaka's moment and her state of mind, the core of the poet's awareness and sense of things.

Her imagery and the mind that propels it run like fast-moving deer through the bracken of language, through thought and emotion, through insight and mystery, through intuition and clear, objective observation. The result of this syntactical energy and rhythm is the creation of numerous passages that have great beauty, gravity and contextual integrity sustained among multiple poems.

This is original, multifaceted, prismatic work. This book is the kind of portal into meaning and understanding that authentic poetry can deliver, and that unrealised verse can never touch or come close to. Over the years, one learns the difference through direct experience with both.

Noriko Tanaka's *From the Middle Country*, her third collection, is a powerful, compelling and exciting new testament to the brilliance possible in the tanka form. Here again, in the hands of a master, the art of tanka demonstrates its ability to adapt and change, to sing the songs that are relevant to a new, more globally oriented, generation.

Michael McClintock
Clovis House
Clovis, California
April 2014

my father
a distant south-sea island,
my mother
gave birth to me
beside the water

I From the Ocean Country: Blue Times

born through the eye
of a needle,
the translucent jellyfish
swims, wobbling
around its world

as a shadow
floating
between life and death
I circled the night
in the aquarium

transparent bodies
of cuttlefish rising
higher and higher –
in the ocean, the blue
of another world

they are like
fast-flowing clouds
schools of sweet smelt
always, forever
fearful of something

whenever the water sac
within my chest
is painful,
my eyes turn into those
of a forlorn fish

my breathing harsh,
I'm gazing upwards –
there is water
in the sky, and
I am a small fish

in my teens, too,
when I suffered nightmares
of dying insane,
there was water
up in the sky

the body of another,
sopping wet –
I think of
what happened next
in last night's dream

following the direction
of the otter, and
a little way behind,
silver bubbles
were rising to the surface

brushing lightly
against one another
and at peace,
there are seals
sleeping the night away

Songs at the Bottom of the Sea

    signs of the witching hour
    approaching :
    in the tank, the tails
    of giant salamanders
    are growing longer

    scattered like
    petals from flowers,
    the red
    of swamp crabs
    crawling along

    slowly wriggling
    their bodies,
    a school
    of minnows goes by
    in front of me

moon jellies,
oh, how chilly must be
the bottom of the water –
when I
think of you

their sleep
is as dismal as death –
in the March water
are floating
sea-otters

from beyond
the aviary hedge
comes a voice saying
'I shall meet you again
in the next world'

'toads
are poisonous, so
I detest them,'
said eyes in the depths
of spectacles

ear pressed to a hole
in the wall, I can hear
now and then
the sea, among the voices
in the neighbouring room

swimming behind
the school of fish,
a single fish
is tangled in foam and
the white shadow of death

as many hairs
as kernels
on corn cobs,
as many lives
as there are deaths

this town has sunk
into the evening gloom –
I am
like a black fish
swimming along

Falling into the Sea

high in the sky
sounds of a sewing-machine
treadling –
rain, you are
a really hard worker

a king penguin,
gazing up at the northern sky,
said
'is this what
life is like?'

moon jellies
shine with dim light
resembling
street lamps
on a rainy day

useless as they are,
those sardines
have precious life
and so they live
as permitted

we are battling
just to survive,
these tufted duck parents
with ducklings
in the water, and I

on the ice
is a seal
lying on its side,
laughed at
for its sexy pose

the shadow of an otter
coming out of the passage
of the aquarium :
its shape is that
of a human child, but…

snapper
in the front of the water tank
as if
I am a fish and
the fish is me

the light bulb
becomes a jelly fish
floating in the room
where my painter friend
lives alone

as forlorn as
winter's blue skies,
the giraffe's ears
twitching
intermittently

there is a time, too,
when I want you
to look at me,
you with a gaze
gentler than that giraffe

in the snow
which drifts along
melting
between sky and sea
is my homeland, I wonder

the closed eyelids
of that lion
fast asleep
on a winter's day…
they look like you

sleeping at night
beside my asthmatic child
I see
in a dream giant trees
beginning to grow

II From the Middle Country: Onogoro Island

I'm thinking about
Onogoro Island
in the 'age of the gods',
meanwhile stirring
some stew in a pot

that old professor
who believe utterly
in dream divination,
is today concerned
by the red of a tomato

in order to meet with
the winter sun and the sea
at dawn
I went swaying along
in the blue train

the deep green
beyond the classroom windows –
I was named
as an example
of 'human nature'

looking
at the water's surface
I am doubtful,
somehow, of whether
I actually exist

as always
I turn for home
at the corner where
there's a shop piled high
with dried bonito

inside my stomach
there is a sun
catching on fire
and also cicadas
crying shrilly

with a single particle
as clue, I'm investigating
several thousand tanka
on this night
of early summer rain

The Sea of Trees

the swallowtail butterfly
that has been riding
the subway with me,
alights at Mikuni Station
and flies away

as a wintry sun
sinks below the horizon
of the sports' field,
I, a mere dot,
am watching

with nowhere to be
I have come by myself
into the thick forest –
that's how I think of
Man'yōshū research

my manuscript
has fallen open
on the floor –
I go to pick it up
from a pool of winter sun

in between
the twilight sky
and the forest,
there is a pocket
for shutting away the sun

writing 'wind'
with our kanji character
I visualise
the fierce wind god
of ancient times

though I read his essay,
I have not yet seen
the writer,
but I label him
a nasty, pompous, man

through the pages
of his essay,
his character is transparent :
he's a dried-up person,
he's a depressing person

it feels as if
this September rain is falling
inside my stomach –
meantime I'm searching
for the book of Kine Island poems

having raised
this plump body of mine
swollen with fluid,
I was researching
the kanji character for 'moon'

is this a sign
I'll become a chrysalis?
recently I have trouble
moving my hands and feet
and do nothing but sleep

Fireflies

the arm
that I stretched out
to no purpose,
was as dark as a street
in the middle of the night

are we fireflies
glimmering in an insect cage?
we sleep
with our little lamps
lighted

hidden away
in the kanji character
for wind
is an insect crying
with a shrrrill voice

amongst the flocks
of clouds flowing
through the sky
this morning, was a cloud
with your name on it

I dream of
raw-green fleabane weeds
sprouting,
and my whole body
turning into a forest

wanting to go
to spring in Hangzhou,
I tried
floating flower petals
in a bowl of water

behind my back
he said 'panda'
three times –
'who's a panda?'
did not I respond angrily

gazing upwards
I see several leaves
of silver foil –
'it's time for me
to take my leave now'

on the window frame
the silver flies of winter –
momentarily
a rainbow arches
behind my eyes

within
the empty bottle
propped
against a wall,
flowed vacant hours

bearing aloft
an umbrella
like a drifting jelly fish
came my friend
from Asuka village

The Tree of Forbidden Fruit

the rain falling
like laundry being done
in a drum,
has been washing me, too,
since this morning

I am always
always
in the midst of
thinking about you
with painful joy

disregarding
the illusion of fish
living in the puddles,
I go over
the pedestrian crossing

that youth
constantly tells me I am
'a nice person' –
in an unexpected twist
the summer sky will come

there are nights
when I think about
the 'Shining Firefly God'
who was revered
in the age of the gods

I was unaware
that from time to time
a path I used
to cross the mountain
was in the clouds

in a lecture
at the beginning of autumn
I heard the theory
that the 'forbidden fruit' tree
referred to tomatoes

every time
I think of you, I
become a leafy forest,
with trees in that forest
swaying in the slightest breeze

there are sparrows
imitating autumn leaves
as the sun
falls headlong
into the dusk

however I call
there is no response –
that cloud is like
my son in the mornings :
'hey!'

in the book
I'll put in the sky
are recorded
the tomorrows
of my worn-out self

III From the Country of the Dead:
   The Sleeping River

when I walk along
wearing a mask
I too am in the dark –
there are sounds
of Darth Vader breathing

the neon lights
of the pachinko parlour are off,
and outside my window
people are going by
wet as weird fish

in front of me
the object of my hatred
gardenias
begin to open
their thick-lipped petals

oh, river
sleeping as you ice over,
there is a blue sky
eternally
disconnected

inside the letter box
it was too dark –
a voice said
'how about putting in
the light from a cigarette'

imagining
the shaggy green grass
is you,
I am nibbling at it
from underneath

to the question
of whether I am
herbivore or carnivore,
I respond by gathering
scarlet fallen leaves

yellow bell-peppers
still green
in patches –
I am nobody's,
not I

in a dream
when I was crying out
to be saved,
only the stardust
looked beautiful

Strange Tales from the World of the Spirits

       beneath a sky
       laid with black felt
       the radio
       pours out strange tales
       from the world of the spirits

       on the table
       where an advance notice
       of murder was delivered
       this morning, I placed
       a red apple, then left

       my older brother says
       he is coming to kill us,
       my child and me –
       somewhere behind him
       Lucifer laughs

is this a street
where monsters mill around?
deep in the night
there's a spontaneous ringing
from the telephone box

the silver skewers
I went and bought,
tonight
threaded with beans,
shine on my dining table

those times
I want to weep
lying on the floor
like a beetle's back,
I fall down prone

when it's too much trouble
to sort out those
misunderstandings,
I go home drenched
with May rain

catching
mysterious radio waves
from outer space,
my right ear aches
on rainy days

maybe because
it's a night of grainy moon,
a dog
is barking in the distance
as if it can't sleep

beyond the dripping
of the rain
are low clouds –
my deceased father's fingers
flick the abacus

on a morning when
I suddenly wanted
to fly through the sky,
I'm going out
with a bat-like umbrella

A Cloud on a Winter's Day

he is a person
with no understanding
of the human heart:
a cloud drifting away
on a winter's day

a morning when
there's a little pot
in my eyes,
which is gradually
filling with milk

I tell myself
not to take any notice –
in the depths
of the winter sky
something makes a sound

awakening
from dreams of a tooth
coming out,
I've peeped in the mirror
these last two or three days

the spring mountain
is fast asleep, when
I hear the sound
of knocking on the door
to the next room

tonight I think
I'd like to hold in my arms
the moon
of Li Bai, the moon
that dwells in the water

in my dream
of an observation tower
noiselessly tumbling,
my bespectacled father
also appeared

I am praised
by someone from eastern Japan
in these terms :
'you don't have much
of a western accent, do you'

I think
of the heat when
his thin eardrums
tremble
at my voice

in the crowded carriage
a person like a bar host
is making
a phone-call,
apparently in tears

when I read poetry
at night in a coffee shop
in the town,
I hear nothing but
voices whispering of love

The Solar Eclipse

when I come up
onto the roof to see
the solar eclipse,
the wind there whispers
'I don't need you'

suspecting a relapse
I walk home
along the embankment –
cicadas without number
are born and appearing there

ah, summer twilight
I sprinkle water
under the eaves –
the one I want to meet
is gone, far away

every night
I see in my dreams buildings
growing taller –
wakening, for a while
I feel my head spinning

at midday
I open the belly of a fish –
coming out
of one cruel dream
I slip into another dream

I laugh, alone,
and suddenly
from the floor
in a corner of the room
a shadow arises

the day winter starts
the sky is brightly coloured –
I pull out
those photographs
you have taken

my shadow reflected
in the winter river –
brightly sparkle
stones whose date and
time of birth are unknown

riding along
the little current
behind a boat
comes a flock of seagulls
with grubby wings

it's the afternoon
for you to come :
fish with silver dorsal fins
are leaping
through the sky

disliking me
he looks away –
spring winds
are continually
carrying the clouds along

A Bird on the Mountain Top

a bird drifts
over the mountain top –
'around there
are air currents, you know'
said my son

calling everything
which drops and scatters,
'spring',
I fall asleep
amidst luxuriant flowers

most of the matters
triggering concern,
have the silence
of stones lying
by the roadside

that afternoon
when the crowd is fascinated
by a rainbow,
one man slips away
and disappears

in the continuation
of my womb-dream,
I stood
on the unlit platform
of an Azusa express

tinier than the dot
made by my pen nib,
is the insect
walking across
the top of my notebook

stroking
the openings
of flat earholes,
gossip entered
into deep pits

Rayleigh Scattering

when asked
'wouldn't you like a kiss?'
the answer
I gave long ago,
was 'yes, sure'

blacking out
my breasts
completely,
there were nights
I made my child cry

wanting only
to hear him say the words
'I love you',
I was gazing up
at the blue of the winter sky

that sky is my past –
meantime
the Rayleigh Scattering
is sparkling
into the distant forever

my blue sky
has now become
an exercise book
for writing your name in,
several hundred times

Snowy Days

within the eyes
of a young man
who's begun talking
of homosexuality,
snow is falling

he was the young man
laughing as he told
the story
of a woman who
was deceived and died

in secret
I have been walking
along the edge of life –
without any trace
trees bear their blossoms

the face of the woman
typing on her keyboard
takes on
a soft expression
this spring afternoon

in my dream
a boy I didn't recognise
appeared
and gave me
a single peach

Blossoms

an emergency staircase
cut off
from anywhere
on planet earth
where flowers bloom

people say
the black cat
is ungrateful,
but it lives on
taking no notice

I desired
love potent enough
to destroy me –
a box filled
with green pears

deep within the house
are hanging white roses,
upside down –
perhaps it would be nice
to live with blind love

as I deceive myself
over and over again,
the aroma
of a sinful apple
spreads through my mouth

Myths and Legends of the Middle Country

discovering
that the world has
such a definite outline,
I peer
through my spectacles

it is said that
the deep sighing
of clams
causes a mirage
in the town where you live

the myth speaks of
a thousand-year-old pheasant
being transformed
by the sea – into that sea
I try setting my right foot

grass grows away
and turns into fireflies :
the legend
I remembered
one rainy night

The Dugong's Bones

they say that
the dugong
leaves behind its bones
while just its soul
has rambling dreams

one could call this
a village with downcast eyes –
rain is falling
and there are not even shadows
from moving creatures

inside my gut
the sun is sinking –
weeping
as she goes along the overpass,
is a solitary child

I've no recollection at all
of being loved –
in my heart
when the wind blows
it's the wind of the grasslands

a flame-like maple –
at times
when I cannot help
but be sad,
I embrace its trunk

From the Country of Forests: Tarō's Condolence Call*

>warming his flute
>in his bosom, Tarō
>went swaying along
>in the steam train,
>to make a condolence call

>beside
>the silent remains
>of the man
>we called 'teacher',
>Tarō sits

>after addressing
>two or three remarks
>to the face of the deceased,
>Tarō leaves
>without playing his flute

* Translators' note: according to the poet, this section was written in homage to her deceased mentor in tanka. The deceased was also mentor to an unusual musician, whose (old-fashioned) given name is Tarō. Tarō is a flute player or, rather, a man who lives to play his flute. Their mutual 'teacher' had praised highly an earlier composition by Noriko Tanaka entitled 'Tarō's Flute'. Hence, 'Tarō's Condolence Call', following on from that, is intended as an elegy for the teacher so venerated by both the poet and the flute player.

he has come back
without meeting and greeting
the guests at the wake,
and is stretched out
alone in his room

thinking about
the way his teacher
pronounced 'h' words,
Tarō was again
playing his flute

tadpoles with legs
are dancing and swimming
in the lotus pond,
amid the sounds
from a flute

he travelled
to the Other World,
wearing ordinary clothes,
whispers Tarō
as he gazes at the moon

a moonlight night
when it seemed that the dead
would come to call,
Tarō takes out and plays
his *fukeshakuhachi*

the voice of the wind
like the sound
of my teacher, whistling –
the mountain frogs
must have been fast asleep

when I turn around
hearing the sound of a flute,
I see that a firefly moon
has appeared
on the mountain-side

From the Old Country: Earth Spiders

>though I called them
>through the mountain ravines
>where the spirits
>of earth spiders sleep,
>my parents did not respond

>in the vicinity
>of the river Sai
>were stones with ears
>which understood
>the language of people

the silent stillness
of mountains mid swirling clouds –
autumn has come
to that hill where
my parents now sleep

I have come back
to my ancestral land, Yamato –
in the afternoon
I call out, but no one
answers in this house

snow is falling,
piling on my spirit,
that spirit which
many times in the past
killed my parents

I Am Not Crying

slipping on
a pair of oldies' spectacles,
I looked through them
seeing that night had fallen
in this crooked world

though a teardrop
was running
down her cheek,
'I'm not crying,'
said my mother

a day when loneliness
wells up like water
in a salt jar –
the island is my father,
the ocean is my mother

putting a lid
on my cup of hot soup,
I think about
this process of rain
falling on the earth

Afterword by Noriko Tanaka

I have still not seen Heaven.
Perhaps that patch of blue sky between floating clouds might be Heaven.
But I have not been there yet.
For human beings there is something called 'one's lot';
and I have a sense there is some kind of world we must not see.

>   that patch of blue sky
>   between floating clouds –
>   I do not know
>   what lies
>   beyond there

Noriko Tanaka
Spring 2013

Noriko Tanaka: A Brief Biography

Noriko Tanaka was born in 1967. In 2008 she was awarded the prestigious Nakajo Fumiko prize for tanka. In 2011 Noriko received a special award from the Kinki block of the Japan Tanka Poets' Society for her excellent tanka collection.

Noriko lectures at Kinki University and Setsunan University. She is a selector for the Honganji Shimpo Tanka Club, and belongs to the following literary societies: the Modern Poets' Association, the Japan Tanka Poets' Society, the Yama Mayu Dōjin Coterie and the Japan Writers' Association.

Her publications include four tanka collections, *Doorway to the Sky* (2008), *Breast Clouds* (2010), *Moon Forest Armada* (2010), *From the Middle Country* (2013), and the books of essays, *An Investigation into Expressions: the Man'yōshū and Contemporary Tanka* (2012) and *Tanka to Eat* (2012).

Doorway to the Sky, *Breast Clouds*, and *Tanka to Eat* have been translated into English by Fielden and Ogi.

www.ingramcontent.com/pod-product-compliance
Lightning Source LLC
Chambersburg PA
CBHW062201100526
44589CB00014B/1896